W9-BTG-214

FOR EVERETT AND JOSEPH

COPYRIGHT © 2005 BY GEOFFREY GRAHN
All rights reserved. Published by Orchard Books, an imprint of Scholastic Inc. ORCHARD BOOKS and design are registered trademarks of Watts Publishing Group, Ltd., used under license. SCHOLASTIC and associated logos are trademarks and/or registered trademarks of Scholastic Inc.

No part of this publication may be reproduced, or stored in a retrieval system, or transmitted in any form or by any means, electronic, mechanical, photocopying, recording, or otherwise, without written permission of the publisher. For information regarding permission, write to Scholastic Inc., Attention: Permissions Department, 557 Broadway, New York, NY 10012.

Library of Congress Cataloging-in-Publication Data
Grahn, Geoffrey. What's going on in there? / written and illustrated by Geoffrey Grahn.— 1st ed.   p. cm.
Summary: Grahnville looks like an ordinary town, but a turn of the page reveals that the pizza cooks are actually building a dinosaur, and many other things are not as they appear. ISBN 0-439-57495-1 (hardcover : alk. paper) [1. Cities and towns—Fiction. 2. Visual perception.] I. Title: What is going on in there? II. Title.
PZ7.G7612Wh 2005   [E]—dc22   2004005195

10 9 8 7 6 5 4 3 2 1   05 06 07 08
Printed in Singapore 46   First edition, March 2005
The text is set in 30-point P22 Johnston Underground.
Book design by Geoffrey Grahn and David Saylor

ORCHARD BOOKS ● NEW YORK

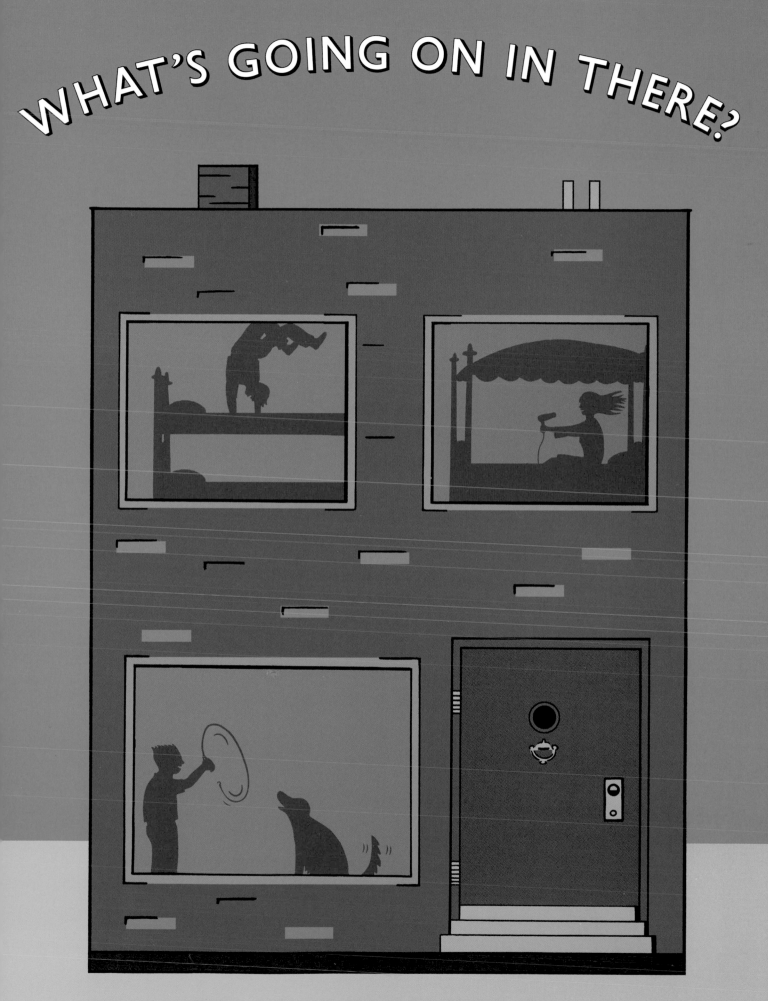

WELCOME TO GRAHNVILLE, U.S.A.

It's an ordinary town, but things are not as they appear. Let's take a walk and see!

WHAT'S GOING ON IN THERE?

Are those boys and girls
taking a test?
(Sssshhhh, quiet!)

No, they're not taking a test.
The drinking fountain overflowed,
so everyone is taking rowing
and swimming lessons.

WHAT'S GOING ON IN THERE?

Are Aunt Martina and her friends pulling saltwater taffy?

No, they're not pulling taffy.
Aunt Martina is planning
a trip to Mars.

But, bringing along some
saltwater taffy would be
a great idea.

WHAT'S GOING ON IN THERE?

Are Dino and his brothers
making pizza?

No, they don't make pizza
here on Thursdays.

Today, Dino, Bronto, Stego,
and Pterry are building
a dinosaur.

WHAT'S GOING ON IN THERE?

Are Derek and Eric getting ready for Christmas?

No, they're not getting ready for Christmas. They're giving Octavio his afternoon bath.

It's always Christmas at Octavio's.

WHAT'S GOING ON IN THERE?

Is Butch getting a haircut?
He'd better hurry or he'll be
late for his karate lesson.

No, Butch isn't getting a haircut. He's watching the circus. Didn't you notice the sign on the door?

(Go back and you'll see.)

WHAT'S GOING ON IN THERE?

Is Eunice feeding her cats?
She sure has a lot of cats.

No, Eunice isn't feeding her cats. She has only one cat and his name is Otis.

WHAT'S GOING ON IN THERE?

Are the Rackets

making dinner?

No, they're not making dinner.
Mr. and Mrs. Racket are playing
tennis. But when they're done,
they'll have pizza for dinner.

Whoops!
Someone should tell them
Dino's Pizza is closed today
because of a dinosaur.

WHAT'S GOING ON IN THERE?

Are the Burr twins having

a pillow fight?

No, they're not having a pillow fight. Someone left the freezer door open, so the Burr family is going on an arctic expedition.

WHAT'S GOING ON IN THERE?

Is everyone asleep?

Yes!

Everyone is asleep.

Good night!